"When someone you love becomes a memory, the memory becomes a treasure."
Author unknown

IN MEMORY OF

My Dad

Add a photo here

"Today, I'm having a hard time with..."

"Today, I remembered..."

"One feeling I've felt coming up a lot lately is..."

"One thing I want to remember about my dad is...."

Describe a memory with your dad that makes you laugh.

Write about where you feel your grief in your body. Where does your grief stay?

Where does your mind go when you let it wander?

"The life of the dead is placed in the memory of the living."
Marcus Tullius Cicero

What is one thing you could try to make today easier on yourself?

When do you feel most connected to your dad?

Write a mantra you can return to when you feel overwhelmed by grief.

What is a way you could celebrate your dads memory?

What memory did you share with your dad that you wish you could relive?

If you could forgive your dad for something, what would it be?

What new stories have you heard about your dad
from family or friends since he passed away?

If you could tell your dad about your day, what would you tell him?

What songs make you think of your dad? What were his favorite songs?

"Perhaps they are not stars in the sky, but rather openings where our loved ones shine down to let us know they are happy."
Eskimo legend

If you could forgive yourself for something, what would it be?

Write about a time you had difficulty getting along with your dad

What is something your dad taught you that affects the way you live your life daily?

"I know this feeling won't last forever because... "

ame something you have learned about yourself.

What are you willing to do/change to help yourself heal?

What are some memories of your dad that make you smile?

Talk about a comforting memory of your dad

"I am ready to feel....."

"If tears could build a stairway, and memories a lane, I'd walk right up to heaven and bring you home again."
Author unknown

How did your dad influence your life?

What are you having a hard time understanding

What are your grief triggers?

_____

_____

_____

_____

_____

_____

_____

_____

_____

_____

_____

_____

_____

_____

_____

_____

_____

_____

_____

_____

_____

_____

_____

"Now you are gone, I am going to..."

What has changed most in your life since your dad passed away?

Write a list of feelings and emotions you wish
to release.

What quote or song reminds you of your dad?

What is something you are struggling to accept?

"The hardest part about you being gone is..."

"Don't cry because it's over. Smile because it happened."
Dr. Seuss

"The most painful part of grief is...."

How do you comfort yourself on bad days?

When you go to bed, what thoughts keep you awake?

What scares you the most about death/loss?

The hardest time of day is...

What are you most grateful for...

Do you have any feelings of guilt, if so, why?

If you had one more day with your dad, What would you spend it doing?

List some ways you can be kind to yourself.

> "A life with love will have some thorns, but a life without love will have no roses."
> Anonymous

Which season is the hardest without your dad, and why?

Is there a certain smell or scent that reminds you of your dad?

How do you choose to remember and honor your dad?

What things have you learned about yourself since the loss of your dad?

"Dad, life without you is....."

10 words that describe your dad

"Dad, when I think about you, I....."

What do you want people to remember about your dad?

If there was a gift in your grief, what might it be?

"To live in hearts we leave behind is not to die."
Thomas Campbell

Which part of losing your dad do you find the most difficult to cope with?

Draw a map of your grief journey, illustrating each stage you experienced along the way.

Describe a "What if" scenario you have been thinking about since your dad passed away.

When was the last time you felt truly happy?

Share the best advice your dad gave you

"Our bond is unbreakable because....."

(Describe the bond you feel with your dad)

What habit of theirs drove you nuts?

In a perfect world, what would you change about your life?

_____

_____

_____

_____

_____

_____

_____

_____

_____

_____

_____

_____

_____

_____

_____

_____

_____

_____

_____

_____

_____

Name three things you are grateful for today.

"Say not in grief 'he is no more' but live in thankfulness that he was."

Hebrew proverb

"Tomorrow, I will wake up and...."

_____

_____

_____

_____

_____

_____

_____

_____

_____

_____

_____

_____

_____

_____

_____

_____

_____

_____

_____

_____

_____

_____

_____

_____

_____

Do you believe that grief and happiness can coexist? Why or why not.

"I feel sad, but I want to feel……"

Besides grief, what other emotions are you feeling?

How is your grief different in public and when you're at home?

Name three people who have helped you
in your grief...

What do you wish someone would have told you about grief?

Explain how grief feels to you...

Share your "grief playlist."...

"The best and most beautiful things in the world cannot be seen or even touched. They must be felt with the heart."

Helen Keller

What is the worst grief advice or cliché you've heard?

Find one of your favorite pictures with your dad. Describe what happened that day.

What is your earliest memory of your dad?

What did he always do to make you laugh?

What is an inside joke or saying that only the two of you would understand?

What activities did you do together?

(Pick at least 1 to describe in as much detail as possible

What sound reminds you of your dad and why? What's your favorite memory associated with this sound?

Talk about a small memory that seems minor/insignificant

Write about a time when your dad
embarrassed you....

"We need never be afraid
of our tears."

Charles Dickens

What dreams or thoughts about your dad have recently come up?

_____

_____

_____

_____

_____

_____

_____

_____

_____

_____

_____

_____

_____

_____

_____

_____

_____

_____

_____

_____

_____

_____

What will you miss the most about your dad

What image do you see when you close your eyes
and think about your dad,

_____

_____
_____
_____
_____
_____
_____
_____
_____
_____
_____
_____
_____
_____
_____
_____
_____
_____
_____
_____
_____
_____
_____
_____

If you could rewrite how you said goodbye,
would you, and what would you do differently?

If your dad was here with you, what advice would he give you for healing after losing him?

_____
_____
_____
_____
_____
_____
_____
_____
_____
_____
_____
_____
_____
_____
_____
_____
_____
_____
_____
_____
_____
_____
_____
_____

Which color reminds you of your dad and why?

If you could speak to your dad again for just a few minutes, what would you say?

If your dad could speak to you today, what would he say?

Take time to thank yourself for taking good care of your mind and body

"Everything that has a
beginning has an ending.
Make your peace with that
and all will be well."

Buddhist saying

Made in the USA
Las Vegas, NV
20 January 2024